The Single Woman's

PRAYER BOOK

SELINA ALMODOVAR

Dedication

This book is dedicated to my husband, Kyle, whose faith in me to produce a good work neither wavered nor fell short. Thank you for bringing out the best of me as a wife, mother, and writer. I am forever grateful for your love, dedication, and for redirecting me at times when I felt lost. You are God's perfect gift to me.

This book is also dedicated to Sissy. It only takes one example of faith to change a life. You were my example. Thank you for walking in the ways of the Lord so I could see that with God, all things are possible. I pray this example will now change the lives of many.

Contents

Dedication i

About this Book 1
   My Golden Ticket 1
   Prayer Works 4

Why a Prayer Book for Single Women? 8
   For the Seasoned Prayer Warriors 12

How to Use This Book 15
   Seeking 16
   Healing 17
   Embracing Singleness 17
   Preparing for Love 17

A Few Other Things 19

Seeking 22
   Prayer of Salvation 23
   Discovering God's Love for Me 26
   Staying Focused on God's Plan 29
   Trusting God 32
   Drawing Closer to God 35
   Praising God Through The Storm 38
   Praising You Through The Wait 41

Healing 44
   Removing Baggage 45
   Prayer of Forgiveness for My Ex(es) 48

Healing from Rejection 52

Healing from all Doubt and Insecurity 56

Healing from Jealousy & Envy 60

Healing from a Victim Mentality 64

Removing Fear of Dating 68

Removing Fear of Mr. Right 71

Removing Fear of My Future 74

Embracing Singleness 77

Single Woman's Daily Prayer 78

Daily Self-Love Prayer 81

Feeling Content.. 84

Finding My Purpose and Direction 88

How to Love Again.. 91

How to Love and Accept Myself.................... 94

How to Trust Myself 98

Prepare My Heart for Mr. Right.................... 101

How to Remain Pure in My Singleness 105

Preparing for Love 109

Praying for Mr. Right 110

Moving Into a New Relationship 114

Trusting In Mr. Right...................................... 118

How to Remain Pure In
a New Relationship 122

Prepare Me to be Wife Worthy.................... 125

Additional Help 129
Now What?.. 130
Notes 133
Afterword... 139

About this Book

My Golden Ticket

In my early 20's, I went through a horrible breakup. It was one of those breakups where you knew that it was a good thing, but it left me completely scared out of my mind as to what would happen next.

In fact, being single and facing this world on my own felt scarier to me at the time than holding onto my very toxic relationship. And believe me, I tried really hard to hold onto whatever was left of it.

Since I was forced to face the world as a single woman, I decided to do what every other girl does in this situation. It's probably what you are doing right this very moment… I decided to focus on "me".

You know exactly what that means. We hit the gym. We start a new devotional to get closer to

God. We turn up the self-love to a level 10 and indulge in doing our nails and getting massages, all while cleaning out that "past" clutter from our personal space. We may invite over more of our friends than usual. Basically, we begin to live the life that seems fun, fancy, and free.

But the truth of the matter is that as much as I wanted to enjoy my independence, I still cried at night over a guy who was no longer in the picture. There are countless breakup songs and I belted each and every one of them. And, like me, you might also feel like being single is cool and all (seriously, it really is), but there's nothing like feeling loved at the end of the night by someone who truly cares for you.

So, before I could truly find myself and heal from my last breakup, I managed to get over my ex by getting involved with a new love, in a new relationship, and a new chance at a happy life.

Now, there were some things that I held onto from my single days (like the devotional time, and the "I can take care of myself" attitude), but of course, I brought all of my baggage, pain, insecurity, and love for my ex, into this new relationship.

It eventually caught up with me after the initial butterflies had flown away. Because I was so committed to making this relationship work, I grew totally dependent on my new boyfriend. I created a new life and future for us before we could ever allow it to develop naturally. While some would call it "psycho", I called it, "preventive planning".

After two years of dating in college, I had already planned out the details to our wedding, names for our children, family vacays, and how we would grow old together. I used my boyfriend as an anchor to the happy life I always dreamed of having.

He was my golden ticket. And there was nothing and no one who could get in our way...

Now, did homeboy feel the same way? Ehhh, not so much. He broke up with me after two and a half years of dating. His reason for breaking up? He had to break up with me. No, I'm not telling you that he had to do it. I'm telling you that was his actual reason. That is actually what he told me before hanging up on me (oh yes, it was done over the phone!).

And then, just as fast as he came into the picture, he was out of it. Never to be seen again. You can imagine how I must've felt at this point.

Perhaps you're feeling exactly how I felt... hurt, embarrassed, confused, dumbfounded, alone, insulted, rejected... I mean, humans with souls just don't do that, right? Christian believers wouldn't hurt others like that, would they??

Yup. They did. He did. And I'm deeply sorry if you have ever experienced a hurt like this.

SELINA ALMODOVAR

Prayer Works

After this breakup, I felt completely defeated. And very scared. And very numb. I entered a phase of depression where I wouldn't eat enough and drank entirely too much. But before I began this season of self-destruction, I did something else. I prayed.

It was a very simple prayer. Seeing as I had very few words to say, but felt a whole lot of feelings, I prayed what I could in the moment that I was in. I remember desperately wanting to be alone so that I could give God a piece of my mind. When I was finally granted that opportunity, I couldn't speak. All I could do was cry and sob.

Yet, I felt as though my heart was speaking for me. There I was, pouring my heart out, reliving every painful moment of that breakup and every other breakup before it. It felt soooo good to get it all off my chest. The pain was so deep that I felt like my eyes were crying to God Himself!

In the end, my actual prayer was summed up in three words: "I trust You". That was all I could manage. And as raw and emotional as my heart was at the time, it meant those three little words with everything it had.

Now, flash forward to another single season. I was self-medicating my breakup as best I could. And just like my previous single season, there was still this… void. This lack of feeling loved.

Don't get me wrong, church and God were very

4

much a part of my life, both when I was in relationships and when I was single. I sought God in songs, devotionals, and through those pretty Pinterest quotes. I believed that God was going to bring me a man worthy of becoming my husband. But because my wounds were so deep, God's remedy was not working soon enough.

So I took matters into my own hands, until God spoke. I went out to clubs and bars. I met nice guys and not-so-nice guys. I was taken for granted, and taken for a fool. I tried to run back to my exes (all of them). Nothing worked. Even though I was doing everything you're supposed to be doing as a single woman, I still couldn't find love. Not in myself, not in others, not in things, nor places, nor money, nor my workout routine. It was nowhere to be found.

I want you to know that I sincerely held onto my three-word prayer as best I could. I felt in my core that God would be the answer and that He would somehow save me from the mess I'd made.

But that's the thing. Here I was, running around town with this victim mindset, "praying" for God to save me, when in reality I needed to be saved from myself. I wasn't making good choices, and because I wanted to control my outcome, I wasn't fully trusting God with my whole heart.

The final game changer was an interview I heard on the radio. An artist had written a song that was inspired by a question. His question was, "If you stood face-to-face with God right now, what would you say, and how would you feel?" I meditated on this for weeks. No matter how many times I went to church, read my devotions, and prayed for miracles to happen, I felt ashamed at the woman I was becoming. I didn't have any words for God. And I didn't want it to be that way.

I wanted to feel so completely comfortable with God that I could just run into His arms. He would spin me around and we would smile, laugh, and all would be great. That's where I wanted to be. That's how I wanted to feel.

That answer left me with a revelation… my relationship with God was downright nonexistent. Sure, I acknowledged that He was there, and I knew by faith that He could change my life, but that was about it. I was doing nothing to turn my belief into a comfortable, loving relationship.

So in 2011, that's what I began to work on. And let me tell ya, that was the missing piece to everything.

So how does a lady like me (and you) create a relationship with God? Through prayer. Seriously. Prayer works and it can change your heart. It changed mine. And I write to you today as a living testimony of that.

I have more peace today than I have ever had in my entire life. I am happily married to my best friend and husband. We have an amazing life together and an awesome baby boy. Being a mom has been the greatest gift I've ever received in life. And to think, I

THE SINGLE WOMAN'S PRAYER BOOK

was ready to give up and throw all of this away because of my lack of faith in what God could do!

The best part? I feel completely comfortable with who I am as a woman, and who I'm becoming. I can honestly say that I know now what real love feels like, because I've been blessed to find it in God, myself, and my Mr. Right. I discovered the keys to lasting love and it all began with prayer.

Prayer works.

7

Why a Prayer Book for Single Women?

When I first had the idea of writing a book, my love story instantly came to mind. This specific chapter of my life has been the most impactful and life-changing chapter to date. My story has become an inspiration for many of my friends, family and coworkers. So much, in fact, that I started a relationship coaching business to help women all over the world find the keys to lasting love for themselves, based on the lessons I've learned throughout my 20's.

Naturally, some sort of autobiography or self-help book should've been the result. But it wasn't. After praying about it (of course), I was reminded of my humble beginnings. I was reminded that without prayer, none of this would even exist for me, or for those whom I inspired over the years.

Since my prayers and faith are what ultimately changed my heart and love life, I felt in my spirit that prayer should be the very first thing I write to you about. I believe that prayer can change your circumstances as it did for me.

There are many prayer books out there for you to dive into, many of which I've used during my season of singleness. Slowly but surely they helped me heal and grow into a woman of faith.

But none of them spoke directly to the pains, needs, and desires of what my heart was going through during that particular time. There were no prayers I could draw to that could help me let go of my ex. Or a prayer to help me keep hope alive when all of my other friends seemed to have their lives together and I didn't. And I found nothing for when I had trouble learning how to trust again…

I believe your single season is uniquely special because it's the greatest time for God to use you! However, the devil knows that, so he does (and is doing) everything possible to mind-ninja us to believe that we'll never truly find Mr. Right, and experience real love. The enemy messes with our confidence, security, and sense of worth so badly that we often lose sight of who's really in charge here, and where love actually comes from.

I'm writing this book for two reasons:
1) To reset the playing field of love
2) To encourage you to develop a deeper prayer life

First, I wanna reset the playing field and put God back in charge when it comes to love, romance, and Mr. Right. If I could look into your eyes right now, I would tell you from the bottom of my heart that if you trust God with everything you have, and live by His standards, then He'll take care of you and this particular area of your life.

> *"But seek first the kingdom of God and all His righteousness, and all these things shall be added to you."*

Matthew 6:33

But you gotta be willing to trust Him and love Him. Did you hear me? You can't just know about God and believe in Him based on what He has done for others. You need to develop and nurture a stronger relationship with Him, and have faith that He's going to do something BIG in your life too! Because He can. And He will. If you let Him.

The second reason I decided to write this book is that sometimes prayer can be a really intimidating thing. When I decided to fully live for Christ back in 2011, I was very nervous about praying. I flat out didn't know how to pray.

To me, it was like being at a group thing, where you had to go around and say one thing about yourself. But you're so freaked out about that one thing that you're supposed to say that you totally ignore what everyone else is saying and you have no idea who is who because you missed all their names. Then, it's finally your turn, and you totally blank out on that one awesome detail about yourself, so you choke and say, "uh, hi... I'm Selina. I... like cats." Ugh. Epic fail.

Then you spend the rest of the group circle time thinking of all the cool things you should have said, and you're kicking yourself, all the while not paying any attention to anyone else, again. The entire activity is a huge disaster, and you're right back where you started.

Yeah, that's how I used to feel about praying. I would get nervous, ignore all of the other prayers, would only consider my own prayer requests, then get so anxious about praying that I would rush through it, only to instantly regret what I said because I could've prayed a much better prayer if I'd just had more time to think about it.

My prayer life was all about making some grand impression to God, then ignoring His time with me because I was too busy overthinking my "performance".

I'm writing this book to change that anxiety in you. While prayer may seem nerve-wracking and intimidating at first, I can assure you that over time, with the right mindset, and perhaps a few prayer examples to help you along the way, you'll have a sense of comfort, peace, and confidence when it comes to prayer with God.

For the Seasoned Prayer Warriors

If you're a seasoned prayer warrior, and you have no fears when it comes to praying, then awesome. You are already way ahead of where I was when I was single. You may have gravitated towards this prayer book not because you have trouble praying, but because you're seeking inspiration on what to pray for.

Sometimes it can be difficult to pray for ourselves, much less to pray over this particular area of our life. God is pretty detailed and very specific. Don't agree? Just look at His instructions for building Noah's ark, or the tabernacle, and don't even get me started on Solomon's temple! I believe that because our God is a God of full and total detail, we must therefore pray in detail as well.

So whenever you're praying about your life, your struggles, your frustrations, it takes more than just, "Lord, bring me a cute husband" to make your prayers count.

"The LORD is near to all who call upon Him, to all who call upon Him in truth. He will fulfill the desire of those who fear Him; He also will hear their cry and save them."

Psalm 145:18-19

Now, don't get me wrong here; God hears everything. Any prayer (even a three-word prayer like mine) that is lifted up in faith is going to count. But I believe that when we take those prayers, and pray them with detail, we begin to open our hearts to expose our truest, most innermost desires. And that is exactly what God seeks: Total communion with you!

So if you know how to pray and it's already a part of your Christian walk, then perhaps my prayer book will inspire you to pray for certain areas of your love life in more detail, so that you can expose a new piece of your heart to your loving Father.

This prayer book is not only going to help you overcome any fears you may have about praying, but it'll also help you gain healing, peace, and the love you've been looking for since forever. I'm hoping that reading my prayers, the very prayers that I prayed when I was in my single season, will uncover something in you that'll spark the breakthrough you need to prepare your life for your next season.

Even better than that, this prayer book can bring you close to God like never before, so that

13

someday, my prayers will evolve into your own personal prayers… in total security, in the presence of our loving, living God.

How to Use This Book

I wanted to make this book as simple as possible for you. While I recommend going through each category in the order that it was written, you can most certainly go to any prayer you want (or need) without feeling like you are out of sequence.

If you need a quick prayer regarding something specific because you're feeling a certain way, then go for it. However, if you are simply looking to use this prayer book as a guided 30-day devotional, where you meditate on one prayer each day for 30 consecutive days, then the beginning will be your best starting point.

There are a total of 30 prayers in this book. They are divided into four categories:

Seeking

Before getting into a relationship with Mr. Right, before getting over your relationships with Mr. Wrongs, there's one relationship you need to focus all of your attention on. And that's the one you have with Jesus Christ. The seeking prayers are written to help you engage in true relationship and deepen your walk with Jesus.

If you've never had a personal encounter with Jesus before, then I can understand how this section would be a bit difficult for you. Receiving God's love is contingent on getting to know Him. And trust me, you're gonna want to receive His love, because it will become your personal blueprint to understand all other loves. If you can truly say that you know what a pure, unconditional, genuine love feels like, then you know that it's real love. You can then find similar qualities of that love when it comes from yourself, friends, family, and perhaps someday, your Mr. Right.

To help you better understand this concept, listen to the audio exercise, "How to Have an Intimate Moment with Jesus" at:

http://selinaalmodovar.com/SWPBResources

Healing

Now that you have sought a deeper relationship with Christ, allow Him to take over your heart and get to work in it. The prayers in this section are meant to soothe your fears, doubts, discouragement, pain, hurt, and more.

Embracing Singleness

As your heart heals and your relationship with Jesus strengthens, you'll feel the need to rediscover yourself. Self-love begins to unfold and you begin to genuinely appreciate yourself! These prayers were written to help you do just that.

Preparing for Love

Trust me when I say there will actually come a time when you will truly enjoy being single. And just when you've reached that point in your life (if you're not there yet), God will bring someone into your life. But you might hesitate to move forward due to past pains, or fear of messing up your cozy life. The prayers in this section are written to help you navigate through this part of your love life. In hopes that it'll lead you to your lasting love with Mr. Right.

Each prayer can be read verbatim, just as they are... however, there are some fill-in-the-blanks to help you make these prayers become your own.

Feel free to read these to yourself and meditate on them. But you know what they say… faith comes by hearing. When you're feeling ready and are comfortable with praying, I encourage you to begin to pray out loud, so that your faith grows.

A Few Other Things

1. Scriptures. There are a few Scriptures that came to mind as I prayed these prayers. Use these as references, verses to meditate on, or as a way to dig deeper into the Word that can be paired with your prayers.

2. Additional Personal Prayers. I want you to use this space to jot down any additional prayer points you may have that I've left out. Really own these prayers. God already knows your heart, so there's nothing really to hide from Him. Writing out your prayers will be like putting all of your cards on the table. You're pretty much exposing all that you have going on in this particular area. When you choose to do that, you are choosing to trust God with it, and you surrender your control over it, which are both really, really good things. So, I encourage you to stretch yourself and utilize this space. Because prayer works. And your personal prayers will work too if you feed them your faith.

You can read through this book in its entirety while jotting down your own personal prayers. Once you've finished, you can go through this book again and come out with a totally new experience because now you have those added prayers! If you need a few pointers on how to create your own personal prayer, you can check out the "Creating Your Own Prayer" handout at:

http://selinaalmodovar.com/SWPBResources

3. **Notes and Answered Prayers.** It is always extremely awesome and rewarding to go back and see how far you've come. It's important to recognize when God has moved in your life because it'll increase your faith, increase your hope, and encourage you to keep going! So, use this section to address any answers you've received from a specific prayer.

4. **Additional Resources.** Because I couldn't just stop here with this book, I wanted to give you a few extra resources that you can use to help you

engage and develop your prayer life while embracing your single season. Go to:

http://selinaalmodovar.com/SWPBResources

to receive handouts, video trainings, and other useful tools that'll enhance this book, your prayer life, and your single season.

Seeking

And you will seek Me and find Me, when you search for Me with all your heart.

Jeremiah 29: 11

Prayer of Salvation

Dear Lord, Creator of all things, heaven and earth… I know that You have also created me. Now I am beginning to understand that You also love me more than anything in this world, because I am one of your most precious daughters.

You love me so much that You sent Your beloved Son, Jesus Christ, to die for my sins.

I know that if I don't choose You and Your love, my sins would eventually lead me to death. Lord, I humbly ask that You forgive me of those sins.

I ask that you forgive me for _____, as well as those sins that I've forgotten.

I choose life with You, Lord. I ask You to come into my heart and fill it with Your unending love. Repair my heart, Lord, in a way that only You can.

I want to embrace Your love and everlasting life for the rest of my life. I thank You Lord for Your love and for increasing my faith to know You better.

Thank You, Jesus, for dying on the cross for my sins, and for rising up again for me. Thank You for your unfailing love. And I thank You for giving me new life!

In Jesus's name,

Amen

Scriptures

If you declare with your mouth, "Jesus is Lord," and believe in your heart that God raised him from the dead, you will be saved. For it is with your heart that you believe and are justified, and it is with your mouth that you profess your faith and are saved.

Romans 10:9-10

Personal Prayers

Notes – Answered Prayers

Discovering God's Love for Me

Lord,

As I sit here today, I am at a standstill. I know that you love me – I know that Your love is there. I know that it is very wide and deep and tall because your Word tells me so. But today, Lord, I'm having a really hard time feeling all that love that You have for me.

More specifically, I'm having a hard time grasping the idea that all of that love could be for me. Right now, I need all of the love that I can get. And it's going to take more than "knowing" about this love of Yours.

God, I want to feel Your love upon me like never before.

Help me to discover it in ways that I've never imagined. Right now, there is a void in my heart and I desperately wish to fill it with You. So I ask You, in this moment, as I rest on my faith, to feel Your love and to know that this love is coming from You.

I give You my heart, O God. It's quite delicate and fragile, but I know that You will take the very best care of it. I pray that you will heal me and bless my heart to be filled with Your everlasting love all the days of my life.

Amen.

Scriptures

For I am persuaded that neither death nor life, neither angels nor principalities, nor powers, nor things present nor things to come, nor height nor depth, nor any other created thing, shall be able to separate us from the love of God which is in Christ Jesus our Lord.

Romans 8: 38-39

Personal Prayers

Notes – Answered Prayers

Staying Focused on God's Plan

Dear Lord,

There is nothing that I want more in life than to please You and give You the glory in all things. I desire to live out the purpose that You have for me. Help me to see what that calling is, Lord.

More so, help me, Holy Spirit, to seek no other plan but Yours. I pray that I will not be tempted with any worldly desires that would cause me to lose sight of your plans. If and when I am being tempted, make my escape route crystal clear to avoid those temptations.

I confess my urge to control my life, especially in the area of _____.

I surrender this to You right now, Lord. I don't know how to get where I need to go but I trust that the end result will be good as long as I am with You. Give me faith to walk out Your plan and purpose with joy and thanksgiving.

I ask for Your abundant wisdom so that I know how to stay focused in all seasons on You as my centerpiece and cornerstone. Lastly, I thank You and praise You for all that You're getting ready to do in my life!

Amen.

Scriptures

But seek first the kingdom of God and His righteousness, and all these things shall be added to you.

Matthew 6:33

Personal Prayers

Notes – Answered Prayers

Trusting God

Dear God,

My intentions are good. I want to trust You with every fiber in me. But sometimes that is the most difficult thing to do! How can I give up control so that I can actively trust You with my life and future?

Help me to do just that. I don't want to have to stress over every detail of my life. I want to give it all to you, Lord. Every single bit of it, including _____.

As I lay down these things that I have been trying to control in my life, I pray that You would mend my heart and forgive me of this sin. Give me the faith to trust Your words, Your promises, and Your plan over my life.

Help me to trust You through the storms and through those annoying silent seasons. Help me to be thankful for all that You've done, are doing, and will do in my life.

I want to put my faith into action– I want to love You deeply. So I trust You.

I trust You, Lord. I trust that You got this. I trust that everything is under Your sovereign control.

Thank you for helping me build this trust with You.

Amen.

Scriptures

But without faith, it is impossible to please Him, for he who comes to God must believe that He is, and that He is rewarder of those who diligently seek Him.

Hebrews 11:6

Personal Prayers

Notes – Answered Prayers

Drawing Closer to God

Dear Lord,

You know that I love You and desire that You be LORD over my life. I also desire to know and love You deeply. I want our relationship to strengthen unlike ever before.

When I read Your Word, I ask to feel Your power in every passage. When I worship, I pray that You remove any and all distractions so that it's just You, me, and our time together.

Help me to love You as a bride loves her groom. Help me to feel and express that deep, forever kind of love. I know that I will never be able to experience this with a man until I am first able to experience it with You.

I want to commune with You on a daily basis. I want my faith and trust to grow, Lord. I want to be like David and be after Your heart.

Show me daily how I can make all this possible. May my thirst for You never run dry. May I be comforted by Your presence daily and may Your daily presence renew my love and joy for You.

Amen.

Scriptures

The LORD is near to all who call upon Him, to all who call upon Him in truth. He will fulfill the desire of those who fear Him; He also will hear their cry and save them. The LORD will preserves all who love Him, but all the wicked He will destroy.

Psalm 145: 18-20

Personal Prayers

Notes – Answered Prayers

Praising God
Through The Storm

Dear Lord,

It's been a tough season. You already know where my heart is at, but I wanted to share this with You personally. My heart is troubled and it is difficult for me to see through this storm.

Help me, Lord, to focus only on You so that I may walk into Your loving arms. Give me the strength to endure these troubles. Holy Spirit, set my heart to worry less and to seek only You.

I know You say to count my joys through the various trials… but Lord, I need Your help with that! Help me to see your joys while I'm facing this storm.

Remind me of Your goodness. I desire to praise You, Lord, as I go through the remainder of my rainy days. I know that You are right here with me and that Your promises are already ahead of me.

I want to give thanks (in the midst of this storm) specifically for _____ .

I know that You are going to help me through this, Lord, so I'm asking for Your peace and comfort right now. Still these rushing waters. Still my worried heart. In Your name.

Amen.

Scriptures

When you pass through the waters, I will be with you; And through the rivers, they shall not overflow you. When you walk through the fire, you shall not be burned. Nor shall the flame scorch you.

Isaiah 43:2

Personal Prayers

Notes – Answered Prayers

Praising You
Through The Wait

Dear Lord,

I come to You, not because of my suffering, but because of my lack of patience. I want to trust Your perfect plan, and I want to feel totally content with it... but I'm finding that lately, it is a very difficult thing for me to do!

Lord, Father of all time, is there any way that you could block the time I am to wait from my senses? Help me to see the lesson in all of this. Better yet, Lord, I ask that You use me during this season of wait. Set me on a road that keeps my mind and heart focused more on You, and less on the time.

Allow me, Lord, to feel Your grace as I sit still. I know that this waiting period is for a good reason.

Forgive me, Lord, for my impatience, anxiety, and frustration. I ask that You speak to me words of encouragement– because right now, I need to be encouraged. I need Your strength and self-control to endure this season.

Help me to see less of me and my will and more of You and Yours. I rejoice in the woman that I will become because of this season!

Thank you for helping me to focus on Your truths.

Amen.

Scriptures

Wait on the LORD; be of good courage, and He shall strengthen your heart; wait, I say, on the LORD!

Psalm 27:14

Personal Prayers

Notes – Answered Prayers

Healing

Then they cried out to the LORD in their trouble, and He saved them out of their distresses. He sent His word and healed them, and delivered them from their destructions.

Psalm 107:19-20

Removing Baggage

Dear Lord,

I'm coming to You to help me do the impossible. I need Your strength tonight. Even though my past is behind me, there are things and people from my past that continue to haunt me. I want to move forward, God, but I don't know how to shake this weight off!

I no longer want to be oppressed by the hurts and pains of my yesterdays. I offer these sacrifices to you, O Lord. I lay down my pains and fears and past at Your feet. Have Your way with them as you have Your way in me.

I pray to become free of any and all baggage that I

am carrying. Search my heart, Lord, for things and people that I need to let go of. Specifically, I pray to let go of _____.

I trust that Your love and goodness will heal me from these old wounds. Help me to not look back and to focus on now instead. Create within me a new, steadfast heart and spirit.

I thank You for breaking these chains and for setting my mind and heart free to love and live again. Thank you.

Amen.

Scriptures

Therefore, if anyone is in Christ, he is a new creation; old things have passed away; behold, all things have become new.

2 Corinthians 5:17

Personal Prayers

Notes – Answered Prayers

Prayer of Forgiveness
for My Ex(es)

Dear Lord,

I pray to live a life that is pleasing to You. I want to make better choices that will help me learn to love and care for myself. I want to draw closer to You and live out Your will. But as I step into my callings and learn to love again, I am reminded of my ex.

Lord, I feel so much hurt and frustration from this (these) man (men) that I can't help but feel offense and resentment towards them. I thought I could forgive _____.

I thought I had the faith in him to see and believe in

this change. But I cannot without You, Lord. I cannot allow him to hurt me any longer, but I need You to make that possible.

O Lord, I am clinging to the edge of Your garments because all the hurt he has caused me has made me weak. And I am so upset at myself, because I feel humiliated and robbed of love and happiness.

Help me, Jesus. Fix me, Jesus. Heal these wounds. Help me to see that better days are ahead. That You have a better love for me instead.

Lord, forgive me for placing all my love in him instead of You. I want to move past this, and I want to move on with You as my center.

Help me, Lord, to forgive _____ for all he's done to me in my life. Specifically, help me to forgive him for _____.

Give me the healing I need to move on from this. Help me to pray for his wellbeing and future – even if I am nowhere in it. Show me, Lord, what my life could be like without him.

Reveal to me Your unending, perfect love. Right now, Lord, I just need to feel Your love. Mend my soul. I want to forgive _____.

I pray, in the name of Jesus, to release my pain, hurt, offenses, bitterness, and hatred toward _____. It will no longer have a hold over me and my life. I pray instead to fill this void with Your love, grace, and mercy.

Thank You, Lord for this time and for Your patience and healing.

Amen.

Scriptures

Let all bitterness, wrath, anger, clamor, and evil speaking be put away from you, with all malice. And be kind to one another, tenderhearted, forgiving one another, even as God in Christ forgave you.

Ephesians 4: 31-32

Personal Prayers

Notes – Answered Prayers

Healing from Rejection

Dear Lord,

I don't know how to say this, but Lord, You know me and You know my heart. It aches from the rejection that I get from others and from my past. I know that this often holds me back and it causes me to miss out on a lot of good things that You make available.

Lord, I pray that You would remove the pain of rejection from my life once and for all. I pray in the name of Jesus that You would cast out any spirit of rejection that may be dwelling within me. Show me, Lord, where I continue to harbor this rejection in my heart so that I may lift it to You and remove it for good.

Take me to Your secret place where I can feel Your love and acceptance. I pray that Your love would flood my insides like a tsunami. Wash over me and show me what it feels like to be adopted by You. I no longer want to feel like an orphan, who will never receive love, nor be liked and accepted.

I know these are just lies from the enemy because he means to keep me down and hold me back. I believe that You have more for me and that I am to receive all the blessings that You have created especially for me.

I ask you, Lord, to shower me with Your abundant love right now. Holy Spirit, remind me of this amazing love whenever I feel rejected. I pray that You set me free from these chains so that I never hold myself back from a good thing ever again.
Guide me to see when the spirit of rejection is trying to take over a situation so that I may not give into it. Thank You, Lord, for Your healing over this area of my life. I am blessed to know that You will never reject me.

Thank You for showing me what a true love is and for reminding me that I already possess that love within me.

Amen.

Scriptures

But certainly God has heard me; He has attended to the voice of my prayer. Blessed be God, who has not turned away my prayer, nor His mercy from me!

Psalm 66:19-20

Personal Prayers

Notes - Answered Prayers

Healing from all Doubt and Insecurity

Dear Lord,

Thank You for allowing me to come to You in my brokenness. You are such a good, good Father. I honestly believe that You love me unconditionally and that You will meet my every need, as You always have. I thank You for never leaving nor forsaking me.

I know that You love me for me, but I confess that I have a very hard time seeing the same thing for myself. Lord, I'm sorry for not being the woman that I know I can be. I confess to You that I live with doubt. I don't always believe that I am worthy of love from a good man or to have a happy love life.

There are times when I feel like this joy will never come. Lord, I also want to confess my insecurities to You. I know these two things are not of You. But these weights are heavy and I am tired. I don't know how to shake them off... but I know that You do!

I pray that You take my yoke and wear it as Your own. I pray for Your deep rest. Lord, I cast out any spirit of insecurity from my mind and heart, in the name of Jesus, and I pray to receive my divine identity as Your royal daughter instead.

Give me the faith to be confident in myself and in You whenever I doubt. I pray that You cast out any doubt from my mind in regard to any area of my life. More specifically, I pray that You remove my doubt of _____ so that I am free to walk out my true purpose and calling.

I pray to receive a steady spirit and that You would renew my mind on a daily basis. Help me to see myself and my life the way that You see it. Thank You, Lord, for showing me Your true light and receiving Your true love.

Amen.

Scriptures

I will praise You, for I am fearfully and wonderfully made; marvelous are Your works, and that my soul knows very well.

Psalm 139:14

Personal Prayers

Notes - Answered Prayers

Healing from Jealousy & Envy

Dear Lord,

I thank You for every blessing that I have in my life. I want to come to You today because there are times when I feel envious for what others have. I confess that there are times when I feel so frustrated at You because I feel like I should've received a blessing that someone else received and it's not fair.

I get so worked up by this, Lord, and I know that this way of thinking and feeling is NOT from You! Help me with this, Lord. Who am I but dust in the wind to question your ways? I confess to You my envy particularly for _____ .

Heal me from this, Lord, so that I do not drive a

wedge between myself, that person, and my future blessings. I know that You are good and just. I believe that if I haven't received my breakthrough yet, then it is for a very good reason.

Help me to pray for _____ instead of feeling envious of them and celebrate with them for their favor and blessings. Help me to feel content in my own walk, and with my own blessings.

Help me, Lord, to realize how good I truly have it and how grateful I should be for all of the blessings that I currently have. That You gave to me because You love me and know what's best for me.

You are my Perfect Provider. I thank You for even blessing me at all. I don't deserve any of it, and I certainly shouldn't complain or feel upset for the things I do not yet have. Create in me a clean heart, O God. I pray to receive a pureness for Your blessings so that I no longer feed on my envy for others and covet the things I do not have.

Lord, thank You for Your blessings, mercy and grace, which are all new to me every morning. Thank You, for Your forgiveness and for helping me to see that my life is good just as it is today. I pray that as I strive to do my part to become a better woman that I remain fixed on Your goodness and our relationship instead of the things I lack.

You build me up… You complete me. You fulfill my every need. With You, I do not lack in any good thing. I pray to feel Your grace upon me and to feel totally secure in my own life, surrounded by all the goodness that You have already given me.

Thank You, Lord.

Amen.

Scriptures

Trust in the LORD, and do good; dwell in the land, and feed on His faithfulness.

Delight yourself also in the LORD, and He shall give you the desires of your heart.

Psalm 37:3-4

Personal Prayers

Notes – Answered Prayers

Healing from a Victim Mentality

Dear Lord,

I am going through a difficult season and I pray that You will see me through it. For most of my life, I have played the victim (as you already know!) and it is because of _____.

My relationships in the past have all failed and have made me feel miserable. But even though each person hurt me in a new way, at the end of the day, I am the common factor in each of those broken relationships.

I don't want to live the rest of my life as though I have

nothing to do with the problem and that it's everyone else's fault as to why I am not happy. Lord, help me to take responsibility for my actions and my choices.

I confess this victim mindset to You right now and I sacrifice it to You as my offering. Mold me into a woman of maturity who can take responsibility for my life when life does not go as it should.

Lord, I pray for Your guidance as You lead me into a fresh new mindset that is mature and full of Your wisdom. I pray to receive Your wisdom, Lord, in full abundance.

I pray against any lies that the enemy tries to tell me or make me believe in order to convince me that I will never see a good turnaround. You are my turnaround! You are my bright side and solution! You are the reason my ending will be good! Praise You, Jesus, for You are already victorious over my life and Your love reigns all over my heart!

As I move forward, I ask that You help me to see that You are sovereign and just. I no longer desire to point the finger at everyone else. Help me to gain a secure mindset so that I can accept my own responsibility and walk into a life of faith, understanding, maturity, and wisdom.

Thank You, Jesus, for helping me through this prayer.

Amen.

Scriptures

And not only that, but we also glory in tribulations, knowing that tribulation produces perseverance; and perseverance, character; and character, hope. Now hope does not disappoint, because the love of God has been poured out in our hearts by the Holy Spirit who was given to us.

Romans 5:3-5

Personal Prayers

Notes – Answered Prayers

Removing Fear of Dating

Dear God,

I believe in my heart that there is someone out there for me. I know that You have my heart's innermost desires in Your hands. I trust that You will make a way for me to receive love from someone special.

But I'm afraid, Lord. I'm afraid to put my heart out there again. I'm afraid of getting hurt. Lord, I ask for Your wisdom and discernment when it comes to letting someone new into my life.

Protect me and my heart from the enemy. I pray for safety whenever I go out on a date. I pray that You would make the way out of my temptations crystal clear so that my Holy Spirit helper draws me towards Your light and away from sin. Guard my heart from lies and deceit.

Strengthen my spirit so that I do not act out of desperation. Help me to give dating a chance... draw me to the right opportunities with the right guys. Open doors that need to be open and close doors that need to be closed.

I trust You, Lord. Banish all fear and doubt that would keep me from Your perfect plan. I thank You for Your ever-present plan. I thank You for your ever-present goodness and guidance.

Amen.

Scriptures

Trust in the LORD with all your heart, and lean not on your own understanding; In all your ways acknowledge Him, and He shall direct your paths.

Proverbs 3:5-6

Personal Prayers

Notes – Answered Prayers

Removing Fear of Mr. Right

Dear Lord,

I pray to find Mr. Right. I want to live a life where I have a man who is right for me by Your will. But I am afraid of who this man might be, where he'll come from, and when exactly he will come. I know that You have this all figured out, so help me to worry less and trust You more. Help me, Holy Spirit, to become the woman I need to be in order to meet my Mr. Right.

I pray for Your wisdom and discernment whenever Mr. Right comes along, so that I know he's worth moving forward with. Help me, Lord, to not rush into things. I need Your patience.

I do not wish to live in fear once Mr. Right comes. Direct my path, so that when the right man comes, I am not flooded with fear and doubt or pride that could draw me away from a good thing. Help me not to compare my future Mr. Right to any of my previous Mr. Wrongs.

Help me to be patient in choosing him so that I am not forcing a man who is not right for me to be the one. Lord, make it so that I am completely at peace, day by day, with the man You choose for me, knowing that Your will be done in this area of my life.

Amen.

Scriptures

Be anxious for nothing, but in everything by prayer and supplication, with thanksgiving, let your requests be made known to God; and the peace of God, which surpasses all understanding, will guard your hearts and minds through Christ Jesus.

Philippians 4:6-7

Personal Prayers

Notes – Answered Prayers

Removing Fear of My Future

Dear Lord,

I am at a loss for a plan over my life. I feel like things keep falling apart… I need Your direction. I have no idea where to even begin. I know that Your truth will light the way on my path– I ask that You shine Your light over my life today.

Lord, I am praying for Your grace and comfort as I cling to You this season. I am so thankful that You are always in control. Help me, Holy Spirit, to be reminded of that on a daily basis.

Lord, I pray for rest and to be restored. What is it that You have planned for me this season? How will it direct me into my next season? Speak to me, O

Lord, of the things I must focus on today. I no longer want to waste my time worried about my future.

Give me the faith I need to know and to trust that whatever will happen, will be by Your mighty hand. I trust You. I love You. I need You. Thank You for meeting my needs and for fighting for my future.

Amen.

Scriptures

Have I not commanded you? Be strong and of good courage; do not be afraid, nor be dismayed, for the LORD your God is with you wherever you go.

Joshua 1:9

Personal Prayers

Notes – Answered Prayers

Embracing Singleness

Nevertheless (s)he who stands steadfast in (her) heart, having no necessity, but has power over (her) own will, and has so determined in (her) heart that (s)he will keep (her) virgin, does well.

1 Corinthians 7:37

Single Woman's Daily Prayer

Dear Lord,

Thank You for a glorious new day! Give me the peace to see Your love and beauty in all that I encounter today. Thank You for giving me Your strength that is renewed daily. Allow me to use it to be confident and courageous in all that I do. I ask for Your wisdom and discernment to make choices that are only pleasing to You.

Holy Spirit, set my calling in clear sight, and allow no distraction to get in my way. I speak against any doubt, fear, or insecurity that may try to steal my joy. I pray to have a forgiving heart towards any hurt or offense that may come. Based on Your Word, I ask that you renew my mind today and free me from any pain, hurt, or lie that the enemy will try to use against me. Remove the junk in my heart and mind so that I can redirect my time and attention to Your love, grace, mercy, and how I can be a blessing to others.

I desire to draw near to Your love today. Prepare me, also, for the seasons to come. Show me how to love You first before I set my heart on anyone or anything else. Allow me to see myself as the beautiful creation You created me to be. Teach me to become her and trust You as You mold me into her.

I choose to give You all the glory on this day, in Jesus's name,

Amen.

Scriptures

Blessed is she who believed, for there will be a fulfillment of those things which were told her from the Lord.

Luke 1:45

Personal Prayers

Notes – Answered Prayers

Daily Self-Love Prayer

Dear Lord,

I come to You today because I desire to draw near to You. I want to get closer to You to feel and receive all the love that You have for me. Lord, I confess that it is often difficult for me to see what You see in me. Help me to overcome that so that I can learn to love myself as You love me.

Show me how I can care and nurture myself the way You desire me to. Allow me to see these practices as pleasing to You. Help me to see your truth and to no longer believe the enemy's lies that tell me self-love is a selfish sin. Remove any loneliness or insecurity that has come from my lack of self-love. Help me to see Your definition of self-love and how I can practice it daily.

Help me to see what I need to do in my life in order to feel loved by You. Make a way so that I can find more time and opportunities to get to know You. Help me daily to get to know myself. Show me what love is supposed to feel like and help me to desire it from You above all things and people.

Lord, I understand that loving myself is something that will help me feel more joy and peace in my life, but I cannot make that possible without Your love. I ask that You renew my faith in this area of my life. I pray to radically transform the way I see love in myself and how I receive it in my life. I ask these things in Your name.

Amen.

Scriptures

For God has not given us a spirit of fear, but of power, and of love and of a sound mind.

2 Timothy 1:7

Personal Prayers

Notes – Answered Prayers

Feeling Content

Dear Lord,

I desire to focus on myself and my relationship with You during my season of singleness. And You know my heart and all that I feel in regards to this. But I am calling out to You, Lord, because I feel frustrated. I do not see myself being where I'd like to be. I wish I could work harder and make better choices for my life.

Lord, I confess that I am living a life of worry. I worry that I will not meet my personal goals or become the woman I see myself as. I worry that I will be alone for the rest of my life because I do not have _____. I know that You don't care about these things and that You love me just as I am. But I have a hard time seeing that for myself.

Help me to see what You see in me. Help me to accept and love myself as I am. Help me to feel content living as the molded clay and allowing You to shape me all the days of my life.

I ask that You show me how to give grace to myself, Lord. I am not perfect and I never will be. This is why I need You. I ask that You remove this image of self-perfection from my heart, in the name of Jesus, and You replace it with a passionate desire for You to perfect me with Your goodness instead.

Thank You, Lord, for loving me just as I am. And for comforting me with a plan that is perfect and special to me. Thank You for blessing me with Your peace and comfort. And for reminding me of all my blessings that are currently within my reach. Help me to stay present and not worry about my past or future. Thank You for your wonderful gift of the present and the blessed assurance that You remain next to me every step of the way.

Amen.

Scriptures

Not that I speak in regard to need, for I have learned in whatever state I am, to be content: I know how to be abased, and I know how to abound. Everywhere and in all things I have learned both to be full and to be hungry, both to abound and to suffer need. I can do all things through Christ who strengthens me.

Philippians 4:11-13

Personal Prayers

Notes – Answered Prayers

Finding My Purpose and Direction

Dear Lord,

I believe that You have called me into a season of singleness because I am meant to grow and be used. I believe that Your timing is perfect, and therefore, I ask that You show me what my purpose is at this time. How are You to use me? What are the lessons I am supposed to be learning during this time?

Lord, I pray for direction over this area of my life. Help me not to set my mind on my relationship desires, but to look at Your bigger picture instead. Who should I be connecting with? Which projects should I be involved with? Do I need to move anywhere in particular? Is there a specific area in my life that I need to focus on?

I trust you, Lord. I know that Your wisdom is abundant. I ask to receive Your wisdom and discernment in the name of Jesus. I pray for direction over my life as I am solely focused on You and Your will. I pray that You will give me all the resources I need to make this all possible. Give me the steps to take day-by-day and the tools and gifts I need to fulfill my purpose.

Lastly, Lord, I pray that You would shut any door that does not need to be open during this season. Let there be no distraction from the choices I am to make at this time. Help me to focus more on You, and less on me. Thank You for Your plans that You have for me, and for the ability to let them come to pass in this season.

Amen.

Scriptures

I will instruct you and teach you in the way you should go; I will guide you with My eye.

Psalm 32:8

Personal Prayers

Notes – Answered Prayers

How to Love Again

Dear Lord,

Finding and feeling love is a very hard thing for me to do. I've been hurt in this area of my life time and time again. I know that this feeling is not of You. I know that You are the definition of the greatest love. I believe that Your love can heal my wounds and make me whole again. I ask that right now over my life.

Help me to know what Your love feels like. May You shower me with Your everlasting love so that it floods my insides to the very depths of my heart. Help me to feel whole and full of love again so that I can learn to love others and myself the way You designed me to.

I pray that You would remove any fear that would block me from giving and receiving love right now. May Your perfect love cast out all fear that lives within me and help me to see Your love as a good thing, meant to heal and strengthen me.

Teach me to love again, Lord. Show me how to love and give me the actions and words to say to pour love into the lives of those around me. Reveal to me what I must do in order to do this. Give me the courage I need, Lord, to allow love to live in me and shine through me once more. I receive Your love right now, Lord, in the name of Jesus. Thank You for Your peaceful, perfect love.

Amen.

Scriptures

Beloved, let us love one another, for love is of God; and everyone who loves is born of God and knows God. He who does not love does not know God, for God is love.

1 John 4:7-8

Personal Prayers

Notes – Answered Prayers

How to Love and Accept Myself

Dear God,

You are such an awesome God! Thank You so much for Your grace and love. For giving me the gift of life where all Your blessings flourish.

Lord, I know from all Your gifts, and from Your countless ways of being there for me, that Your love for me is unconditional. There is no doubt that I have regarding Your love for me. But when it comes to loving myself, I find it hard to feel the same way.

Lord, I am so unworthy of Your love. Thank You for Your unending grace and mercy that loves me regardless of my worth. There is so much that I wish I could do differently. I am constantly judging myself and it is exhausting.

Teach me to love myself, O God. Help me to accept myself as I am. Show me the ways that I can establish love for myself so that I can live life feeling the love that You have created for me. Let me not focus on the darkness of myself– I pray to shift my eyes, mind, and heart to focus on Your light in me instead.

I know I'm not perfect... I don't know why I keep striving for this perfect version of myself. I know that You made me with a purpose and that You don't make junk. I pray that You break the chains of perfection in me and help me to feel love for myself and accept myself completely.
Where I feel that I am weak, I pray that Your perfect strength will make me strong. Wherever I feel dissatisfied with myself, I pray that You give me the wisdom and boldness to do better, but to do so with joy in my heart and love in my spirit.

Help me to fill my void with You and Your fruits. Thank you, Lord Jesus, for always loving on me and for never giving up on me.

Amen.

Scriptures

Do not let adornment be merely outward—arranging the hair, wearing gold, or putting on fine apparel—rather let it be the hidden person of the heart, with the incorruptible beauty of a gentle and quiet spirit, which is very precious in the sight of God.

1 Peter 3:3-4

Personal Prayers

Notes – Answered Prayers

How to Trust Myself

Dear Lord,

I want to live the best life I possibly can while being single. I want to walk away from this season as a mighty woman of God. I want our relationship to strengthen in such a way that I never imagined.

However, I am worried about getting there. Lord, I've placed my trust in all of the wrong people and things, and because of that, I can no longer fully trust in myself to make the right decisions. Help me, Lord, to regain confidence in myself and in my choices.

I pray to lean only on You this season. Holy Spirit, show me when opportunities arise to draw near to you so that I can trust in You with all of my mind, heart, body, and spirit. Show me, Lord, the woman that You have created me to be so that I can know her and love her fully.

Lord, I pray that I am not tempted to think less of myself when it comes to living a lifestyle that is better for me and my future. Give me the patience and grace I need to learn exactly how to trust in myself. I know that in order to trust myself, I must learn to trust in You.

I thank You for giving me that chance this season. Thank You for choosing me to become something great as I continue moving forward to become the best me ever.

Amen.

Scriptures

Now may the God of hope fill you with all joy and peace in believing, that you may abound in hope by the power of the Holy Spirit.

Romans 15:13

Personal Prayers

Notes – Answered Prayers

Prepare My Heart
for Mr. Right

Dear Lord,

I desire a husband. I want to live a life where a man whom You have called to be my husband would love me deeply and wholeheartedly for the rest of my life. I know that to be a wife worthy of one of Your sons, I must be prepared to fully walk in Your ways.

I pray that You would use this season of my life to prepare my heart for my Mr. Right. Show me any roots of offense, fear, discouragement, doubt, shame, neglect, selfishness, or regret. By Your Holy Spirit, I pray that You remove them from me in the name of Jesus.

I ask for Your healing to wash over me so that I can replace those things with Your fruits instead. Prepare my heart to be filled with Your love, joy, peace, patience, kindness, goodness, gentleness, faithfulness, and self-control. Open doors in my life that will help me learn how to become an excellent wife.

Bring mentors into my life whom I can look up to and will hold me accountable according to Your ways. Give me Your gift of wisdom and discernment for when I am ready to pursue a man to love.

Lord, I've tried to do this my way, and I failed horribly. I want to now do this Your way. Show me how and bless me with Your grace as I walk in Your ways.

Free me from any tempting thoughts that would cause me to be led astray. Remove from my heart any thoughts of confusion when it comes to feeling attraction for the wrong men, the opposite sex, or married men.

I feel like I'm ready for this chapter of my life, but if I am not, then please address this in my heart so that I may be content to fully trust and follow You.

Thank you for the Mr. Right You are molding for me.

Thank You for Your guidance and Your lessons on love that will bring me closer to Your love and Your perfect gift for me: my Mr. Right.

Amen.

Scriptures

He has made everything beautiful in its time. Also, He has put eternity in their hearts, except that no one can find out the world that God does from beginning to end.

Ecclesiastes 3:11

Personal Prayers

Notes – Answered Prayers

How to Remain Pure in My Singleness

Dear Lord,

Thank You for making modesty somewhat of a fashionable thing these days. I know that if I wanted, I could dress in a pure fashion… so please help me to desire this. Not only in my clothes, but in my thoughts, attitude, and behavior as well.

There is so much temptation to express my sexuality in the world today. I do not desire to do anything of the sort. Show me that I can appear attractive and confident in my own skin without exposing myself sexually. Help me, Lord, to turn away from sexual desires, thoughts, and entertainment (from books,

TV shows, radio, internet, songs, movies, social media, language, pictures, and anything else my heart can think of.)

Remove this urge in me to want to tap into my sexuality until the right man comes along and we make it official. Blot out any thoughts or feelings of curiosity that I may feel growing in me when it comes to finding love or feeling loved by other women and/or men and replace those thoughts with strength to remain pure and dreams of my wedding night with my future Mr. Right, whom You have called.

Take away any shame that I have lingering in my mind for impure thoughts I have had in the past from sexual thoughts, images, acts, and words. I know that these thoughts do not define me or my future. I want to be a confident bride on her wedding night, not a woman filled with regret, confusion, or fear that I am not pure enough to be someone's wife.

Lord, I pray that You show me a way to fall in love and grow a relationship without sex. Show me how to feel good about myself without putting myself and my body out there.

Help me to find this lifestyle doable and not impossible. Give me a spirit of boldness and courage whenever someone tries to tempt me to live an impure life. Give me a way out of any and all situations that would pressure me to make the wrong decisions. Place in my heart the people, places, books, movies, shows, songs, and lifestyles that I must remove from my life so that I can be cleansed and restored moving forward. I know that great blessings come from great obedience and I want to be obedient in this particular area.

Help me to do just that.

In Jesus's name,

Amen.

Scriptures

I beseech you therefore, brethren, by the mercies of God, that you present your bodies a living sacrifice, holy, acceptable to God, which is your reasonable service. And do not be conformed to this world, but be transformed by the renewing of your mind, that you may prove what is that good and acceptable and perfect will of God.

Romans 12:1-2

Personal Prayers

Notes – Answered Prayers

Preparing for Love

Create in me a clean hurt, O God, and renew a
steadfast spirit within me.

Psalm 51:10

Praying for Mr. Right

Dear Lord,

You know I'm often praying to meet my Mr. Right one day. And I know deep in my heart that one day You will let our paths cross. I cannot wait for that day to happen!

But Lord, I trust You and I trust in Your plan. I know that there is a good reason why I'm single now and am living in this current single season.

So while I'm making the most of my singleness, I want to pray to draw closer to You in every way possible. For that reason, I want to pray for my Mr. Right.

Lord, You know who this man is. You have known him since he was in his mother's womb. Lord, I lift this man up to you today and I ask that you show him how to prepare his heart and future for me to become his wife. Wherever he is, make him have a heart that is after Yours.

May he learn and know to treat others with kindness and may his faith in You be unwavering. I pray, Lord, that he is strong enough to deal with his baggage before ever meeting me. I pray that he is mature enough to live a long life with me without the drama of the world. Lord, I pray for his whereabouts and his safety.

I lift up this man to You, God, and I ask that he would be blessed with a spirit of discernment so that he knows exactly how to love me in the way that I need to be loved.
O Lord, I desire to meet this man so much. I pray that wherever he is, whatever he is doing, that he is thinking and praying about me also. May our hearts draw closer together as we both draw our hearts closer to You. Thank You in advance for this future blessing.

Amen.

Scriptures

Delight yourself also in the LORD, and He shall give you the desires of your heart.

Psalm 37:4

Personal Prayers

Notes – Answered Prayers

Moving Into a
New Relationship

Dear Lord,

Thank You for bringing me this new guy. I really like him and I feel in my heart that it could be something real. Lord, I wanna lift up my friendship with _____. I ask for clear direction on whether I should move forward with this relationship.

Guard my heart, O Lord, and keep me from making any foolish decisions. I pray that You close any doors that need to be closed and that You give me clear confirmation if I am to move forward.

I ask for Your wisdom and discernment to help me make this decision. Search my heart, Lord, for any red flags that I may have overlooked within this friendship. Reveal to me the names of the women I should seek counsel from before I make this thing official.

Lord, You know how much I want this relationship to be real… but not by my will. May YOUR will be done!

Protect me, O Lord, from getting my heart broken all over again. I don't want to waste any more time with guys who aren't serious about a committed relationship. So if you see that this is where my friendship with _____ is going, I pray that You reveal that truth to me right now.

I trust in Your ways, Lord. I pray to be still and not move forward until I hear from You. If this friendship is to move forward, then I pray that I don't sabotage this! May it be that my nerves don't get the best of me. Make our foundation firm and special. Cover it with Your blessings and favor.

Ok, I'm getting excited! Thank You for allowing me to seek You first and to rest in Your comfort. I receive Your peace. Thank You for Your continued care over my life.

Amen.

Scriptures

And this I pray, that your love may abound still more and more in knowledge and all discernment, that you may approve the things that are excellent, that you may be sincere and without offense till the day of Christ, being filled with the fruits of righteousness which are by Jesus Christ, to the glory and praise of God.

Philippians 1:9-11

Personal Prayers

Notes - Answered Prayers

Trusting in Mr. Right

Dear Lord,

Your love for me is so great. You know every corner and inch of my heart. So You already know how deep my feelings are for _____. I have grown to really care for him and I want this to go to the next level.

Lord, I feel that You have been leading me to this man for some time now, and there is nothing that I want to do to ruin it. But, You know my heart, Lord. And You know that I'm finding it super hard to trust him with all of my heart.

Because what if he breaks it? What if he mistreats it? I can't go through another breakup, God. No matter what _____ does to melt my heart, I cannot allow my guard to go down and fully trust him.

Lord, help me to trust in this man. I want to trust in him because I trust in You and I feel that this relationship is good in Your eyes. If it is not, please reveal it to me immediately!

Lord, I pray that You speak to my heart and show me what is rooted in my heart that is keeping me from wanting to trust in _____. Is there something from my past that I must deal with? Or is there a red flag that I simply did not focus on? I pray for Your discernment, so that I can seek the problem and receive Your healing and direction as the solution.

I pray for peace to move forward, Lord. And if I cannot feel Your peace, then I'll know that this relationship is not of You. Help me in this area of my life, Lord. I ask these things in Your name,

Amen.

Scriptures

Your word is a lamp to my feet and a light to my path.

Psalm 119:105

Personal Prayers

Notes – Answered Prayers

How to Remain Pure in a New Relationship

Dear Lord,

I thank You for establishing this relationship between _____ and I. I pray that we can maintain a growing union that would honor You. As we grow closer to each other, I pray that You will forever remain at the center of it all.

Lord, I pray that You will help us to remain pure in our relationship. Give us strength in our spirit to overcome our fleshly desires. Help me to remain modest in how I dress and be cautious in what I say or do with _____.

Even though we are attracted to each other, I do not want to push any boundary too far. Lord, give us a crystal clear way out if any temptation arises. Guard our hearts so that we do not give into our sinful desires.

Help me to discover the heart of this man as I allow him to discover mine. Protect our hearts, minds, and spirit from the enemy and give us strength to continue doing a good work in each other. Allow us to build each other up and not tear each other down. May we be able to fully respect one another, dismiss our own selfishness, pride, or independence, and seek humility from You. Purify us from the inside out.

Amen.

Scriptures

Flee sexual immorality. Every sin that a man does is outside the body, but he who commits sexual immorality sins against his own body. Or do you not know that your body is the temple of the Holy Spirit who is in you, whom you have from God, and you are not your own?

1 Corinthians 6:18-19

Personal Prayers

Notes – Answered Prayers

Prepare Me to be Wife Worthy

Dear Lord,

I pray to become a wife to a godly man. Help me to understand fully what this means. Prepare my heart for such a task. Lord, by Your will, may I find favor in Your eyes to receive such a blessing as this.

Search my heart for what needs to be worked on. Teach me how to become a helper to a husband, and how to happily submit to my future husband. Help me respect him at all times and to know exactly how to love him always.

Show me what I must work on now in this season so

that I not only draw closer to You, and become the woman You have called me to be, but so that I can also fill my heart and mind with good, healthy thoughts, instead of the frustrating, anxious thoughts that I always seem to have.

I pray that You would set my mind on godly things and keep me from feeling as though this moment will never come. You know my heart, Lord. You know that I desire to have a husband. So prepare me for that season, and give me faith daily to trust that this will come to pass by Your hand.

Bring wise women into my life that can help me prepare for this role. I pray to learn as much as I can now so that when Mr. Right comes along, I will be ready.

Lord, as Your bride, I pray that You help me to see husband qualities in You first and foremost. Help me to understand and accept the unconditional love that You have for me before I receive it from my future husband.

Help me to adjust my lifestyle plan so that I know exactly what I must do to prepare my heart, mind, body, spirit, finances, and lifestyle for a life-long marriage with a man You have chosen for me.

Thank You, Lord, for blessing me with this season of

singleness so that I can focus on preparing myself to be wife-worthy.

Amen.

Scriptures

That He would grant you, according to the riches of His glory, to be strengthened with might through His Spirit in the inner man, that Christ may dwell in your hearts through faith; that you, being rooted and grounded in love, may be able to comprehend with all the saints what is the width and length and depth and height—to know the love of Christ which passes knowledge; that you may be filled with all the fullness of God.

Ephesians 3:16-19

Personal Prayers

Notes – Answered Prayers

Additional Help

You did it! You've made it to the end of this book! I pray that it was everything you had hoped it would be, and more!

If you didn't get a chance to check out the additional resources, then check them out now! Go to:

http://selinaalmodovar.com/SWPBResources

and you'll discover audio lessons, handouts, and articles to supplement your prayer book experience.

Now What?

Now that you've completed this book, you might be asking yourself, "What now?" Here are several options you have:

1. **Read it again.** Because the Word tells us to never cease our prayers, you can start again on page one and pray over your single season all over again! And, if you completed the personal prayer section in each of the prayers, then you'll experience a totally new and different prayer month then when you read this the first time. Not to mention, you can add any answered prayers you may have had along the way.

2. **Seek more.** If after reading this book, you felt an urge to seek more help in your love life and single season, then perhaps checking out my Relationship Coaching services is your next step. As a Relationship Coach, I help women find love. First in God, then in themselves, and finally in Mr. Right!

While I spend the majority of my time with single women, the support should not (and does not) end once you get into a relationship. Actually, I would say that you'd need the support then more than ever! If you're single or you've gone exclusive with someone special, and you'd like to receive support, guidance, and clear direction on how to build and sustain your love-life foundation (so that it lasts!) then I would love to become your new Coach!

Go to: http://selinaalmodovar.com/nextstep to set up a time to talk about your options in getting the next step support that you need!

3. **Pass it along.** Let's start a movement! There are dozens of women that you already know in your inner circle who may be going through something that this book can help them with. Start a small group and

experience the book together. Or, simply get this book into the hands of your favorite girlfriends. They say, "hurt people hurt people"; well, the same can be said about "healed people heal people". If you had an awesome time reading this book, and praying these prayers, then care and share.

4. **Tell the world.** If this book was a total game changer for you and you just have to share it with someone (anyone!), then tell the world! You can always check out my Facebook page to share your experience in a post, or you can write a review on Amazon. Those always help, and it'll spark the next girl to take a leap of faith (as you once did) and get this book and start praying!

Notes

Notes

Notes

Notes

Notes

Notes

Afterword

On behalf of every person who has ever pointed out my gift for writing, encouragement, worshipping, or speaking into the lives of other women, thank you. You saw this book in me waaaay before I ever mustered the courage to see it in myself. Thank you for your prayers and your faith in what God could do in me.

God has placed you each onto my path for His glory. This book is not mine, but ours. I pray that it will reach the multitudes and transform the hearts of women in this spiraling time.

If you read this book and your heart was touched, then know that I've been praying for you for a very long time. I pray that you are blessed by it and that God's glory will reach a higher glory from the lives that will be changed and inspired through you.

By faith, God is doing a new thing in you. This book was just a sign towards the way in your wilderness that He has already made. It is the stream in your wasteland. A new generation is upon us. And it begins with you.

Thank you for your faith in me for reading this book, and thank you for your faith in Christ to take care of the rest.

52115622R00082

Made in the USA
Middletown, DE
16 November 2017